Science Dictionary
of the
HUMAN BODY

Second Edition

by James Richardson
illustrated by Gil Hung

This second revised edition published in 2001.

Copyright © 1992 by RGA Publishing Group, Inc.

Published by Troll Communications L.L.C.

Printed in the United States of America.

10 9 8 7 6 5 4 3

abdomen   (AB-doe-men)

The part of the human body containing the stomach, small and large intestines, liver, pancreas, gall bladder, and other organs.

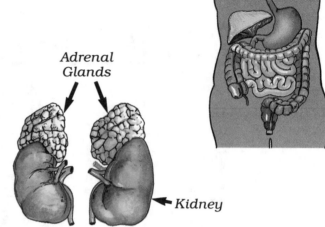

adrenal glands   (uh-DREE-nal)

Glands that make adrenaline. An adrenal gland sits on top of each kidney.

Adrenal Glands

Kidney

adrenaline   (uh-DREH-nuhl-uhn)

A hormone released from the adrenal glands that helps the body prepare to meet a crisis or threat. Adrenaline stimulates many parts of the body, including the heart and lungs.

alimentary canal   (al-ih-MEN-tair-ee)

The pathway that carries food through the body. A continuous tube over thirty feet long in the average adult, the alimentary canal runs from the mouth to the anus.

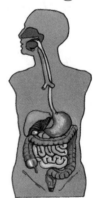

alveoli   (al-VEE-o-lie)

Tiny sacs at the ends of the tubes that carry air into the lungs. Oxygen passes through the alveoli's thin walls into the blood, while carbon dioxide from the blood passes into the alveoli. The singular of *alveoli* is *alveolus*. See **bronchus** illustration.

amino acids   (uh-MEE-no)

A special group of organic compounds that contain nitrogen. Long chains of amino acids make up proteins. Protein in food is broken down into amino acids during the digestive process.

anatomy   (uh-NAT-o-mee)

The physical structure of living things, or the study of such structure.

ankle   (AN-kul)

A gliding hinge joint that joins the foot to the lower leg.

antibody   (AN-tih-bahd-ee)

A protein produced by certain white blood cells. Antibodies help defend the body against invading germs and viruses.

anus   (AY-nus)

The end portion of the alimentary canal.

anvil   (AN-vul)

A small bone in the middle ear, also called the incus. Vibrations pass from the eardrum to the hammer to the anvil on their way to the inner ear. At the inner ear, these vibrations are interpreted as sound. See **middle ear** illustration.

aorta (ay-OR-tuh)

The largest artery in the body. The aorta carries oxygenated blood away from the heart to all areas of the body, except the lungs. The lungs receive blood from the pulmonary (PULL-mo-nair-ee) arteries.

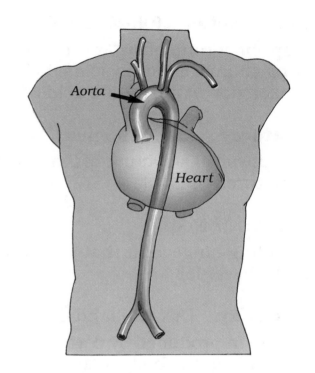

appendix (uh-PEN-diks)

A narrow tube, three to four inches long, shaped like a small worm. It is closed at one end and attached to the large intestine at the other. The function of the appendix is still not clearly understood, but humans can live without it.

artery (AR-ter-ee)

A blood vessel that carries blood from the heart to other parts of the body. Arteries have thick, muscular walls to help pump the blood through the body.

atrium (AY-tree-um)

One of the upper two chambers of the heart, also called auricles. The plural of *atrium* is *atria*. The atria pump blood into the ventricles, the lower chambers of the heart.

auditory nerve (AW-dih-tor-ee)

The nerve that carries information from the inner ear to the brain.

auricle   (OR-ih-kul)

One of the upper two chambers of the heart, also known as atria. The outside part of the ear is also called the auricle.

axon   (AK-sahn)

A long arm of a neuron, or nerve cell. The axon is primarily responsible for conducting nerve impulses away from the cell body. See **neuron** illustration.

baby teeth

A child's first teeth, also called milk teeth or deciduous (deh-SEH-joo-wus) teeth. There are only twenty baby teeth. They start to appear when a child is six to eight months old.

backbone

A series of thirty-three hollow bones, called vertebrae (VER-tuh-bray), that protect the spinal cord. There is a cushion of cartilage between each vertebra and the next. As a person ages, some of the vertebrae can fuse, or join together. The backbone is also known as the spine or spinal column.

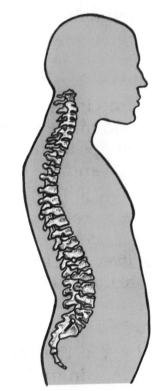

bacteria   (bak-TEER-ee-uh)

Small one-celled organisms that can be seen only with a microscope. Some bacteria are helpful to humans, but others cause disease.

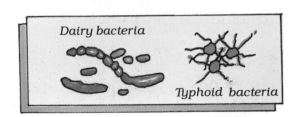

Dairy bacteria

Typhoid bacteria

ball-and-socket joint

A type of joint between two bones that allows circular movement. For example, in the arm, the rounded end of the upper arm bone fits into a socket in the shoulder bone, making it possible to move the arm in many directions. Another important ball-and-socket joint joins the upper leg and hip.

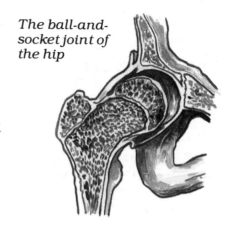

The ball-and-socket joint of the hip

biceps   (BY-seps)

Large muscles found in the front of each upper arm and in the back of each thigh. The biceps in the arms flex the elbow joints and the ones in the legs flex the knee joints.

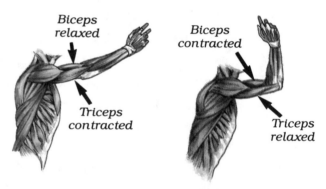

Biceps relaxed

Triceps contracted

Biceps contracted

Triceps relaxed

bile

A liquid from the liver that aids in the digestion of fats. Bile is stored in the gall bladder, a tiny pouch on the surface of the liver.

bladder

A small sac, or bag, in the body that contains fluid. The urinary bladder receives and temporarily stores liquid waste from the kidneys.

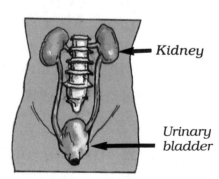

Kidney

Urinary bladder

blister

A watery pocket of liquid under the skin. A blister can be caused by a burn or by material rubbing against the skin.

blood

The fluid that flows through the heart, arteries, veins, and capillaries of the circulatory system. Blood, which is made up mostly of plasma and red and white blood cells, carries nourishment and oxygen to all body parts. The blood also carries away such waste products as carbon dioxide from all body parts.

blood pressure

The force that moves blood through the blood vessels of the body. This pressure is created by the pumping action of the heart. Blood pressure varies in humans according to a person's age and health.

blood vessel

Any tubelike passageway through which blood travels. Blood vessels include arteries, veins, and capillaries. Arteries carry blood away from the heart; veins carry blood toward the heart; and capillaries join arteries to veins.

bone

The hard tissue that makes up most of the skeleton. The outside portion of bones is made of minerals (chiefly calcium), and the inside is made of softer, living tissue called the marrow.

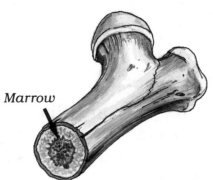

Marrow

brachial artery   (BRAY-kee-ul)

An artery that carries blood from the heart to the arm.

7

brain

An organ located in the skull that consists of nerve cells and supporting cells called glia (GLEE-uh). All incoming information, such as that from the eyes and ears, is received and processed by the brain.

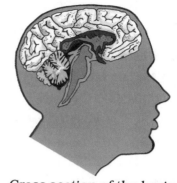

Cross section of the brain

brain stem

The base of the brain, which connects the brain to the spinal cord. The brain stem controls automatic functions such as breathing, heartbeat, and digestion.

breastbone

See **sternum**.

bronchus   (BRONG-kus)

One of two short, wide tubes that connect the windpipe with the lungs. The plural of *bronchus* is *bronchi* (BRONG-kee). Air is breathed into the lungs through the bronchi.

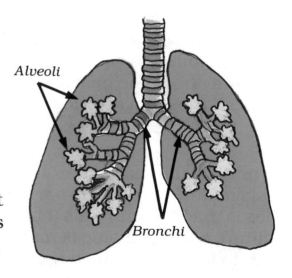

Alveoli

Bronchi

bruise   (BROOZ)

A closed injury in which the skin is not broken. When a person is hit or bumps into an object, tiny blood vessels break below the skin and leak blood into the surrounding area, producing a bruise.

calf

The fleshy back part of the lower leg, which contains large muscles.

capillaries   (KAP-ih-lair-eez)

Blood vessels that connect arteries with veins. The walls of the capillaries are very thin and allow molecules of food, oxygen, and other substances to pass through them to nourish and cleanse all cells of the body.

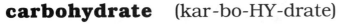

Calf Muscle   *Artery*   *Vein*   *Capillary*

carbohydrate   (kar-bo-HY-drate)

One of the three basic types of food molecules. Carbohydrates are high-energy foods, such as sugars and starches.

cardiac   (KAR-dee-ak)

Of, near, or pertaining to the heart. Cardiac arrest is another term for heart attack.

cardiac muscle

The heart muscle. The contraction and relaxation of the cardiac muscle pumps blood throughout the body. The steady pumping of the heart is the heartbeat. The heart contracts at an average rate of seventy to seventy-five times a minute.

Cardiac muscle

cartilage   (KAR-tih-lij)

Tough, elastic body tissue that makes up part of the skeleton. It covers the ends of bones where they meet in joints. It also forms the ears, the tip of the nose, and the ends of the ribs.

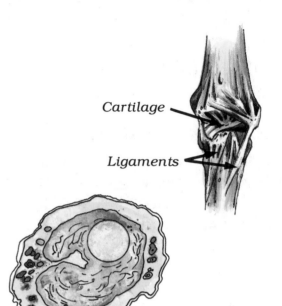

Cartilage

Ligaments

cell

The smallest unit of living matter that makes up all living things. Cells vary in shape and size according to the jobs they do. The human body has trillions of different cells.

cell body

The central part of a neuron containing the nucleus of the cell. Dendrites and the axon branch outward from the cell body. See **neuron** illustration.

central nervous system

The brain and spinal cord. Messages in the form of electrical and chemical signals travel to and from the central nervous system along nerve pathways.

cerebellum   (ser-uh-BEH-lum)

The part of the brain that controls muscle coordination and certain other vital processes. It is located between the cerebrum and the medulla.

Cerebrum

Cerebellum

Medulla

Cross section
of the brain

cerebral hemisphere
(se-REE-brul HEM-ih-sfeer)

One half of the brain. The brain has two cerebral hemispheres, one on the right and one on the left.

cerebrum   (suh-REE-brum)

The largest portion of the brain. The cerebrum is divided into two hemispheres and covers the rest of the brain. Scientists believe that most thought processes take place in the cerebrum.

chromosomes   (KRO-mo-somz)

Tiny, paired, threadlike objects in the nucleus of a cell. Chromosomes are made of a substance called DNA. Sections of chromosomes are called genes.

circulatory system   (SIR-kyoo-luh-tor-ee)

The system of blood, blood vessels, and the heart that carries blood throughout the body.

clavicle   (KLAV-ih-kul)

One of the bones forming the shoulder, also called the collarbone. It is a narrow, curving bone that lies across the top of the chest.

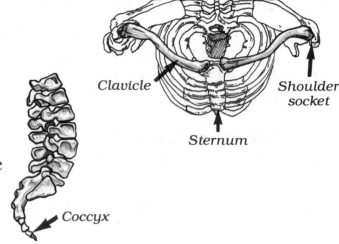

Clavicle

Shoulder socket

Sternum

coccyx   (KOK-siks)

The tailbone. It sits at the end of the spinal column and is formed from four small vertebrae fused together.

Coccyx

cochlea   (KOK-lee-uh)

A part of the inner ear. Shaped like a snail shell, it contains the auditory nerve endings that make hearing possible. See **inner ear** illustration.

collarbone

See **clavicle**.

cornea   (KOR-nee-uh)

The clear membrane that covers and protects the eye. The cornea allows light to enter the eye. See **eye** illustration.

cortex   (KOR-teks)

The outer portion of an organ or body part. The cerebral cortex is the outermost layer of cells in the brain. The outer layer of a bone is also called the cortex.

deltoid (DEL-toyd)

A powerful triangular muscle located on top of each shoulder. The deltoids help control the movement of the arms.

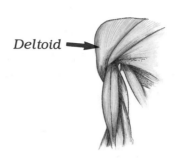

Deltoid

dendrite

A treelike, branching arm of a neuron, or nerve cell. Dendrites usually conduct nerve impulses toward the body of the neuron. See **neuron** illustration.

dental caries (DEN-tul KARE-eez)

Cavities in the teeth; tooth decay. Dental caries are caused by plaque (PLAK), a film on the teeth that contains bacteria. As the bacteria grow, they produce an acid that dissolves the enamel of the teeth.

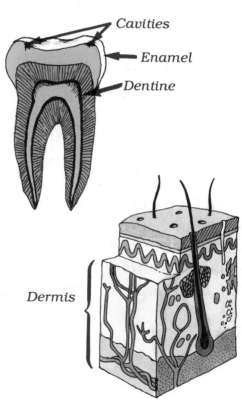

Cavities

Enamel

Dentine

Dermis

dentine (DEN-teen)

A bonelike substance that makes up the inner part of each tooth. It is protected by an outer layer of enamel.

dermis

The sensitive inner layer of skin, also called the cutis or corium.

diaphragm (DY-uh-fram)

The strong, thin wall of muscle that separates the thoracic cavity from the abdomen. The diaphragm aids in breathing.

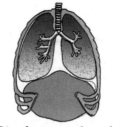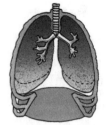

Diaphragm relaxed, lungs deflated *Diaphragm contracted, lungs inflated*

digestion (dy-JES-chun)

The process by which food is broken down into a form that can be used by cells. Digestive enzymes are produced in the pancreas and released into the small intestine, where most digestion occurs.

digestive system

The group of organs and glands that break down and absorb food. The digestive system includes the salivary glands, the alimentary canal, and the pancreas, liver, and gall bladder.

disease (dih-ZEEZ)

Abnormal functioning of the body. Disease may have an external cause, such as infection, or an internal cause, such as a body part malfunctioning. Measles, mumps, and chicken pox are all diseases caused by infections. High blood pressure and diabetes are diseases caused by internal failure.

disk

Any thin, flat circular plate. Vertebral disks are located in the backbone. They are made of a tough, spongy cushion of cartilage and fiber. These disks help the vertebrae move freely and act as shock absorbers for the spine.

DNA

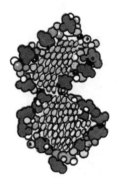

The abbreviation for *deoxyribonucleic acid*. DNA is found within most cells of the body, and it carries the genetic information necessary for cell reproduction.

duct

A tube or passageway, such as a tear duct, that usually carries a fluid or secretion.

duodenum   (doo-oh-DEE-num)

A part of the small intestine. Ten inches long, it is the first part of the small intestine to receive the mixture of food and digestive fluids called chyme (KYME) from the stomach. Digestive juices from the pancreas are also released into the duodenum.

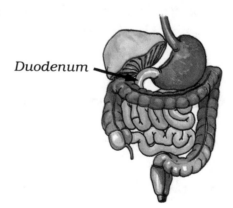

Duodenum

ear

The part of the body that senses sound. It is made of the outer, middle, and inner ear. Small organs in the inner ear also sense the body's position and help keep it in balance.

ear canal

A short tubular pathway in the ear. Sound vibrations travel into the outer ear, through the ear canal, and to the eardrum.

eardrum

A thin layer of skin at the end of the ear canal stretched tightly over the opening between the outer and middle ear. Sound vibrations that hit the eardrum are passed through the bones of the middle ear to the inner ear.

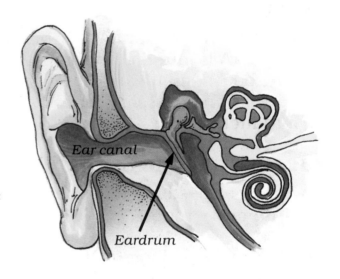

Ear canal

Eardrum

elbow

The hinge joint in the arm where the upper and lower arm meet. The humerus bone in the upper arm and the radius and ulna bones in the lower arm join at the elbow joint.

endocrine gland   (EN-duh-krin)

Any gland that releases hormones directly into the bloodstream. The adrenal, pituitary, and thyroid glands are all endocrine glands.

enzyme (EN-zym)

A protein that controls chemical reactions in the body. Enzymes do many jobs, including fighting infection and aiding in the digestive process.

epidermis (ep-ih-DER-miss)

The two outer layers of skin that cover and protect the body. The tough, dead cells of the epidermis overlap and form a tight, waterproof barrier.

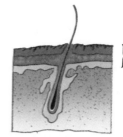

Epidermis

epiglottis (ep-ih-GLOT-us)

A small flap of tissue located at the entrance to the larynx (LAIR-inks). It helps prevent food from entering the trachea (TRAY-kee-uh), or windpipe, when swallowing.

esophagus (eh-SOF-uh-gus)

A part of the alimentary canal. It is a hollow tube that curves from the back of the mouth to the stomach.

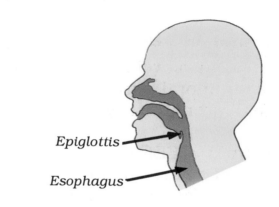

Epiglottis

Esophagus

eye

The sensory organ responsible for vision. Its many parts include the retina, cornea, lens, pupil, iris, and optic nerve.

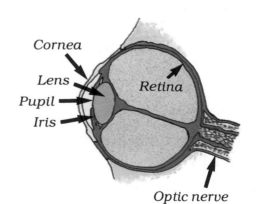

Cornea

Lens

Pupil

Iris

Retina

Optic nerve

fat

One of the three basic types of food molecules. Fats contain more energy than either proteins or carbohydrates, the other two food types, and do not dissolve in water. Cream, butter, and oil contain fats.

femoral artery   (FEM-or-ul)

The large, main artery located in each thigh. The femoral arteries carry blood from the heart to the legs.

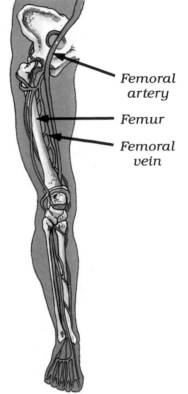

Femoral artery

Femur

Femoral vein

femoral vein

The central vein located in each thigh. The femoral veins carry blood to the heart from the legs.

femur   (FEE-mer)

The bone in the upper part of the leg. It is the largest, heaviest bone in the body. The femur fits into a socket in the hipbone. This ball-and-socket joint makes it possible to walk, run, and jump.

fiber

Any thin threadlike structure. Muscles are made of bundles of muscle fibers that can shorten and lengthen.

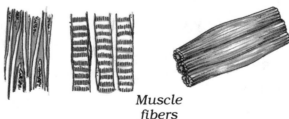

Muscle fibers

fibula (FIB-you-luh)

The smaller of the two bones in the lower leg. It meets the tibia, or shinbone, just below the knee and just above the ankle.

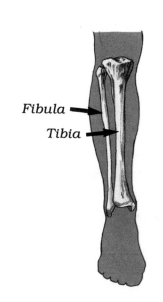

Fibula

Tibia

fluid

Any substance that will flow, such as water or blood. All fluids take on the shape of their container. Gases and liquids are both fluids.

foot

The part of the leg below the ankle, including the heel, arch, and toes. There are more than twenty different bones in each foot.

forearm

The section of the arm between the wrist and the elbow. The forearm has two major bones, the radius and the ulna, and more than six major muscles.

fracture

A break or crack in a bone.

Fracture

freckle

A brown spot of concentrated pigment in the skin. In some people, exposure to the sun can make freckles appear.

funny bone

A spot on the back of the elbow through which the ulnar nerve passes. Hitting this spot stimulates the ulnar nerve, causing a funny, tingling sensation.

gall bladder

A tiny sac on the surface of the liver that contains bile. Bile is released into the small intestine and aids in the digestion of fats.

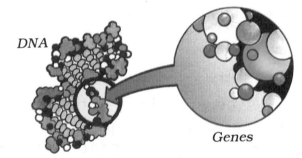

gastric juices   (GAS-trik)

A mixture of acids and enzymes released by the stomach to aid digestion.

gene   (JEEN)

A section of DNA that controls an inherited characteristic, such as the color of one's eyes or hair. All of a child's genes come from the parents.

germ

A tiny living organism, such as a virus or bacterium, that can cause disease. Some germs are so small that they cannot be seen, even with an optical microscope.

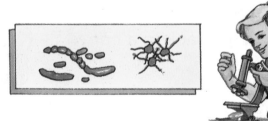

gland

An organ that produces substances designed to perform special jobs in the body. There are two kinds of glands: endocrine and exocrine. Endocrine glands, such as the thyroid, release hormones into the bloodstream. Exocrine glands, such as the sweat glands, release their product through a canal or duct onto the skin or into a body cavity.

goose bumps

Tiny bumps on the skin that appear when one is cold, afraid, or excited. They are caused by the contraction of tiny muscles in the skin that make hairs stand up.

hair follicle   (FOL-ih-kul)

A small pouchlike opening in the skin that contains the root of a hair.

hammer

A small hammer-shaped bone in the middle ear, also called the malleus (MAL-ee-us). Sound vibrations travel from the eardrum to the hammer, to the anvil, and then to the stirrup. See **middle ear** illustration.

head

The portion of the body above the neck, containing the brain and chief sense organs. The main bone of the head is the skull.

heart

The muscular organ in the chest that pumps blood throughout the body. The heart is divided into four chambers, two ventricles and two atria.

heartbeat

The sounds made by the heart each time it contracts. The sounds come from the closing of valves between the chambers of the heart.

hemoglobin   (HEE-muh-glo-bin)

The red protein pigment containing iron that is found in red blood cells. An important component of blood, hemoglobin transports oxygen to body tissues.

hinge joint

A joint that bends like a hinge on a door. The elbow and knee are hinge joints.

hip

The curved portion of the body between the thighs and the waist. The hip supports the backbone and anchors the hipbone, or pelvis.

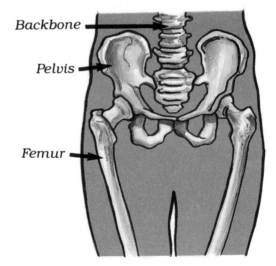

Aorta

Right atrium

Left atrium

Right ventricle

Left ventricle

Cross section of the heart

Backbone

Pelvis

Femur

hormone (HOR-mone)

A chemical substance produced by glands and released into the bloodstream. Hormones control many functions, including growth, reproduction, and digestion.

humerus (HYOO-mer-us)

The bone in the upper arm. One of the strongest bones of the body, it attaches to both the shoulder and the lower arm bones.

Humerus

hypothalamus (hy-po-THAH-luh-mus)

An area at the base of the brain that helps control body temperature, metabolism, and other automatic functions.

immune system (im-YOON)

The body's system for fighting infection and disease. The most important parts of this system are the several types of white blood cells. These cells locate and destroy invading germs and bacteria.

Three types of white blood cells

Bacterium comes close to cell   *Cell opens up and surrounds bacterium*   *Cell absorbs and destroys bacterium*

infection

An invasion of the body by bacteria or viruses that may cause disease. White blood cells fight off the invasion by surrounding, absorbing, and destroying the foreign cells.

inferior vena cava

(in-FEER-ee-or VEE-nuh KAY-vuh)

A large vein that returns blood to the heart from the lower body. The inferior vena cava joins the heart at the right atrium.

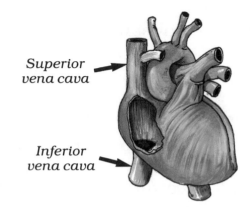

Superior vena cava

Inferior vena cava

inner ear

A liquid-filled cavity within the skull that contains the endings of the auditory nerves. Sound vibrations create movements in the liquid of the inner ear. The movements stimulate the nerve endings. These nerves then send messages to the brain, which interprets them as sound. The inner ear also contains nerve endings that detect body position and help maintain balance.

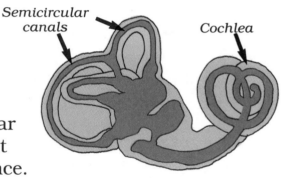

Semicircular canals

Cochlea

insulin   (IN-suh-lin)

A hormone released from the pancreas during digestion. Insulin regulates the amount of sugar in the blood.

intercostal muscles   (in-ter-COS-tul)

Short muscles between the ribs, which raise and lower the rib cage to aid in breathing.

involuntary muscle   (in-VOL-un-tair-ee)

A muscle that works automatically. The heart and the iris of the eye are involuntary muscles.

iris

The circular, colored part of the eye, which is made of muscle. The iris contracts and relaxes to control the amount of light entering the pupil of the eye.

Iris in
dim light

Iris in
bright light

jaw

The portion of the skull that encloses the mouth and contains the teeth. The lower jaw is also known as the mandible (MAN-dih-bul). It is the only part of the skull that can move. The upper jaw, the maxilla (macks-IL-uh), does not move.

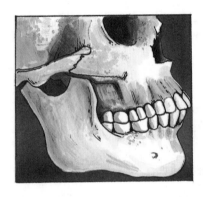

joint   (JOYNT)

A connection between two or more bones. There are many different kinds of joints, including the ball-and-socket, as found in the shoulder; hinge, as in the knee; pivot, as in the neck; gliding, as in the wrist; and suture (or fixed), as in the skull. Most joints are lined with cartilage.

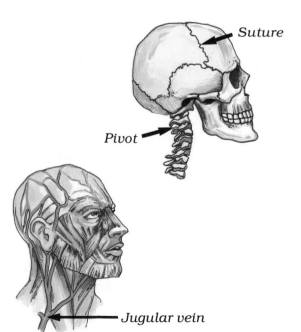

Suture

Pivot

jugular vein   (JUG-yuh-lar)

A large vein in the neck that carries blood from the head to the heart.

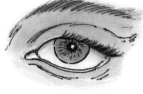

Jugular vein

kidneys

The two organs that filter the blood. The kidneys excrete the waste products of metabolism through the nephrons. The kidneys also regulate salt and potassium levels in the blood.

knee

A hinge joint where the upper and lower leg meet. The femur bone in the upper leg and the tibia and fibula bones in the lower leg join at the knee joint.

kneecap

See **patella**.

large intestine   (in-TES-tin)

The last section of the digestive tract, also known as the colon. The contents of the small intestine pass into the large intestine, which absorbs most of the remaining water. The rest of the material leaves the body as waste.

larynx   (LAIR-inks)

The upper part of the trachea. The larynx contains the vocal cords and is protected by a small band of cartilage called the Adam's apple.

lens   (LENZ)

The part of the eye behind the iris that focuses incoming light on the retina. See **eye** illustration.

ligament   (LIH-guh-ment)

A strong band of tissue that holds bones together and connects joints.

liver

The largest organ of the body. The liver is located in the abdomen and performs many jobs. For example, it aids in digestion, defends against disease, and cleanses the blood.

lower leg

The portion of the leg between the knee and ankle. The two main bones of the lower leg are the tibia and fibula. The largest muscles of the lower leg are called the calf muscles.

lumbar nerves   (LUM-bar)

Five pairs of nerves in the lower back originating in the spinal column.

lungs

Two spongy, saclike organs used for breathing. Located in the chest cavity, the lungs contain millions of alveoli. In the alveoli, the blood absorbs oxygen and gets rid of carbon dioxide.

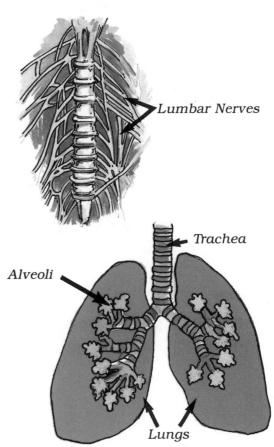

Lumbar Nerves

Trachea

Alveoli

Lungs

lymphatic system   (lim-FAT-ik)

A system of vessels and glands that collects protein outside of the blood vessels and returns it to the circulatory system. The lymphatic system also plays an important role in defending against disease.

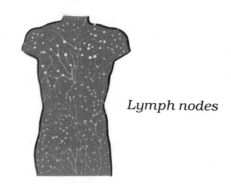

Lymph nodes

lymph nodes   (LIMF)

Small, glandlike structures connected to lymph vessels. Lymph nodes produce disease-fighting cells, called lymphocytes (LIM-fuh-sites), and also purify the fluid carried by the lymphatic system.

lymph vessels

The network of vessels that connects the lymph nodes and carries a clear fluid called lymph.

mandible   (MAN-dih-bul)

See **jaw**.

marrow   (MAR-oh)

The soft inner part of bones. Blood cells are produced in the marrow of certain bones. See **bone** illustration.

medulla   (muh-DULL-uh)

The inner or central portion of a
structure or organ. In the brain, the
medulla, also called the medulla
oblongata, controls automatic
functions, such as breathing and
heartbeat.

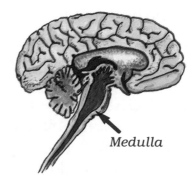

Medulla

Cross section of brain

metabolism   (muh-TAB-uh-liz-um)

The process by which food, oxygen, and all other substances
needed by the body are converted into energy for the body's
use. The waste products of metabolism are eliminated from the
body.

middle ear

An air-filled cavity within the skull
that contains three tiny bones known
as the hammer, anvil, and stirrup.
These bones transmit sound
vibrations from the ear canal to the
inner ear.

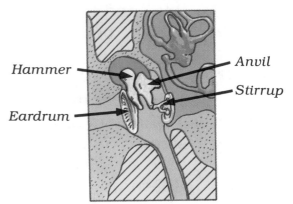

Hammer

Anvil

Stirrup

Eardrum

mouth

The hollow cavity surrounded by the jaws and teeth. The
mouth forms the beginning of the alimentary canal.

mucus   (MYOO-kus)

A thick fluid produced by the body to moisten and protect it.
Mucus lines the mouth, nose, air passages, and intestines.

muscle (MUSS-ul)

A specialized tissue that can shorten or lengthen in response to nerve impulses. Muscles produce motion, support the body, and help keep body temperature constant by producing heat. There are three types of muscles in the body: smooth, skeletal, and cardiac.

muscular system
(MUSS-kyuh-ler)

The framework of muscles that supports the body. Muscles and nerves work together to make the body move.

nasal cavity (NAY-zul)

A mucus-lined chamber in the nose through which air enters the upper respiratory system.

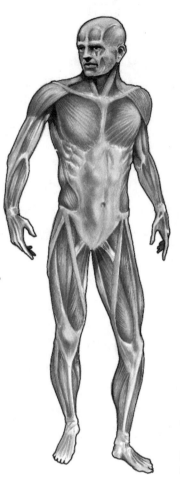

The human muscular system

nephron (NEF-ron)

The part of the kidney that excretes waste. Each kidney has about one million nephrons.

nerve

A fiber or group of fibers that carries electrical signals between the brain or spinal cord and other parts of the body.

neuron (NOO-ron)

An individual nerve cell. Each neuron has three main parts: the cell body, treelike fibers called dendrites, and a group of long fibers called the axon. Information is collected by the dendrites, processed by the cell body, and passed along by the axon.

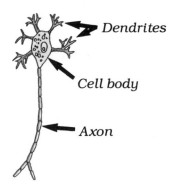

Dendrites

Cell body

Axon

oil glands

Glands located in the skin that release an oily or fatty substance. Oil glands keep the skin moist, soft, pliable, and water resistant.

olfactory nerves (ol-FAK-tor-ee)

Nerves that carry information from the nose to the brain. The endings of the olfactory nerves are tiny hairlike structures lining the nasal cavity. These tiny hairs detect chemicals in the air and send information to the brain, which identifies the odors.

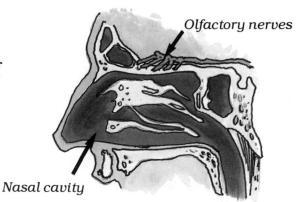

Olfactory nerves

Nasal cavity

optic nerves (OP-tik)

Nerves that carry information from the eyes to the brain. The endings of the optic nerves line the retinas. When stimulated by light entering the eyes, these nerve endings send information to the brain, which interprets the data as images.

organ

A part, or unit, of the body, such as the heart, liver, or kidneys, that works somewhat independently and has a specific function.

outer ear

The ear canal and the soft flexible structure, called the auricle, surrounding the outer opening of the ear canal. Sound vibrations enter the outer ear and travel to the eardrum.

oxygen   (OKS-ih-jen)

An odorless, colorless gas that makes up about one-fifth of the earth's atmosphere. Oxygen is needed by every cell in the body and is used to release energy from digested food.

pancreas   (PAN-kree-us)

A large gland near the stomach that produces hormones and digestive juices. The pancreas releases insulin, a hormone that regulates the amount of sugar in the blood.

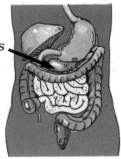
Pancreas

parathyroid glands   (pair-uh-THY-royd)

Small glands that lie near the thyroid gland. They manufacture a hormone that regulates the amount of calcium absorbed by the body.

parotid glands (puh-RAH-tid)

A pair of salivary glands located below each ear. The parotid glands become swollen when a person has the mumps.

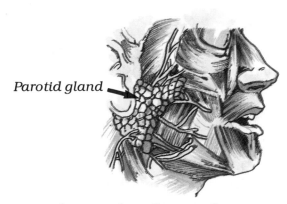

Parotid gland

patella (puh-TEL-uh)

A rounded bone, also known as the kneecap, located in front of the knee joint. It protects the knee from injury.

pectoralis major (pek-tor-AL-is)

A large, thick fan-shaped muscle that spreads from the collarbone down to the outside of the breastbone and across the sixth rib on either side of the chest. This muscle aids in upper-arm movements.

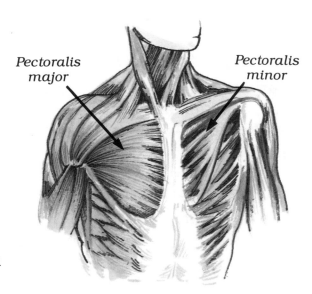

Pectoralis major

Pectoralis minor

pectoralis minor

A thin, triangular chest muscle that helps move the shoulder. The two pectoralis minor muscles are located under the pectoralis major muscles on each side of the chest.

pelvis (PEL-viss)

A large bowl-shaped bone in the trunk of the body, also known as the hipbone. It connects the spine to the legs. See **hip** illustration.

pepsin   (PEP-sin)

An enzyme released by the stomach that aids in digestion by breaking down protein.

pharynx   (FAIR-inks)

The passageway from the mouth to the throat. When food is swallowed, it leaves the mouth and enters the pharynx, then travels to the esophagus.

Pharynx

pigment

A substance that gives color to something. Dark spots and freckles on the skin are caused by a pigment called melanin.

pituitary   (pih-TOO-ih-tair-ee)

A gland at the base of the skull, also known as the master gland. The pituitary produces hormones that control growth, reproduction, water balance, and the functions of many other glands.

platelet   (PLATE-let)

A special blood cell with no nucleus. Platelets stop the flow of blood from a cut or scrape. When a blood vessel is injured, nearby platelets become sticky and form a clot to stop the bleeding.

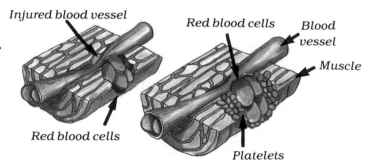

Injured blood vessel

Red blood cells

Blood vessel

Muscle

Red blood cells

Platelets

pores

Small openings in the skin through which liquids can pass.

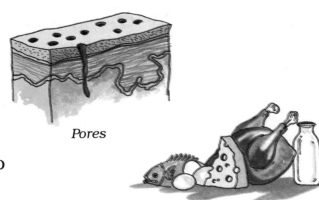

Pores

protein   (PRO-teen)

One of the three basic types of food molecules. Proteins are made of amino acids and contain nitrogen.

pulmonary arteries   (PULL-muh-nair-ee)

Arteries leading from the heart to the lungs. All blood pumped by the heart is carried by the pulmonary arteries to the lungs, where the blood picks up oxygen and drops off carbon dioxide. The oxygenated blood returns to the heart, then passes through the aorta to the smaller arteries of the body.

pulse

The rhythmic movement of blood through a blood vessel. An easy place to feel the pulse is at the neck on either side of the voice box. The pulse rate and the heart rate are the same.

Take pulse here

pupil

The round, dark opening in the center of the iris. The iris opens and closes the pupil to control the amount of light entering the eye. See **iris** illustration.

quadriceps   (KWAD-ruh-seps)

The major muscle in front of the thigh. It helps move the legs and balance the body.

radius   (RAY-dee-us)

The outer of the two bones in the forearm.

red blood cell

A blood cell that has no nucleus and contains hemoglobin, a substance that can carry oxygen. Red blood cells are also called erythrocytes (ih-RITH-ruh-sites).

Ulna

Radius

Red blood cells

White blood cells

respiration   (res-puh-RAY-shun)

The process by which oxygen is inhaled and converted to energy by the body, and carbon dioxide, the waste product, is exhaled.

respiratory system   (RES-puh-ruh-tor-ee)

The system that controls the exchange of oxygen and carbon dioxide in the body. The air passages, lungs, rib cage, and diaphragm are part of the respiratory system.

retina   (RET-in-uh)

The membrane of the eye that is chiefly responsible for vision. The retina receives light images from the lens, then sends the information to the optic nerve. See **eye** illustration.

rib

A bone that curves forward from the spine to enclose and protect the thoracic cavity.

rib cage

A bony cage that encloses the chest, protecting the lungs and heart. There are twelve pairs of ribs in the rib cage. Some are connected by cartilage to the sternum in the chest.

rib muscles

See **intercostal muscles**.

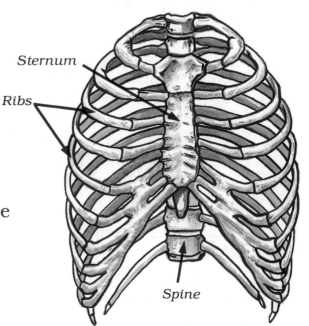

Sternum

Ribs

Spine

saliva   (suh-LY-vuh)

A fluid secreted into the mouth by the salivary glands. Saliva keeps the interior of the mouth moist, lubricates food, and begins the process of digestion.

salivary glands   (SAH-luh-vair-ee)

Three pairs of glands in the mouth, which secrete saliva. Saliva keeps the interior of the mouth moist, lubricates food, and begins the process of digestion.

scapula (SKAP-yuh-luh)

A large triangular bone on the back of the shoulder, also known as the shoulder blade. The scapula joins the humerus of the upper arm in a ball-and-socket joint that has a wider range of movement than any other joint in the body.

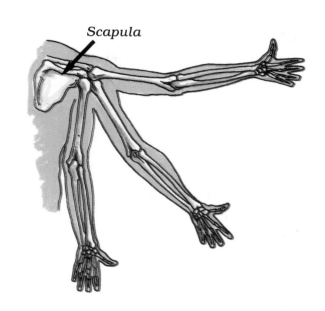

Scapula

scar

A mark or blemish on the skin that forms after a cut or wound has healed. Scar tissue is made of collagen (KOL-uh-jin) fiber, which fills and closes an open wound.

semicircular canals (sem-ee-SIR-kyoo-lar)

Three loop-shaped, fluid-filled canals in the inner ear that help to keep the body in balance. Each canal is lined with nerve endings that sense the position of the fluid and send this information to the brain. The brain interprets this and signals certain muscles to make adjustments needed to stay in balance. See **inner ear** illustration.

shoulder blade

See **scapula**.

sinus (SY-nus)

A small cavity in the body. The nasal sinuses are air-filled cavities in the skull.

skeletal muscle   (SKEL-uh-tul)

Muscle that is attached to bones. Skeletal muscles are usually red in color and are responsible for all voluntary body movements. Skeletal muscles are made up of numerous small muscle fibers.

skeleton

The bony framework that supports the body and gives it shape. There are about 206 bones in the human skeleton.

skin

See **dermis**, **epidermis**.

skull

The bony structure that holds and protects the brain and gives the head its shape. The skull is made up of twenty-two bones fused together.

small intestine

The part of the digestive system that receives the mixture of food and digestive fluids, called chyme (KYME), from the stomach. More than twenty feet long, the small intestine breaks down and absorbs the nutrients of food.

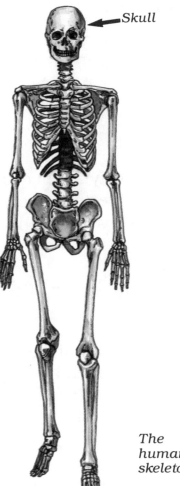

← Skull

The human skeleton

smooth muscle

A type of muscle found in the hollow organs of the body, such as the blood vessels, air passages, and intestines. Smooth muscle, which is usually white, helps the body perform involuntary functions such as digestion.

spinal canal

A tubelike pathway formed by successive openings in the vertebrae of the spine. The spinal cord passes through the spinal canal.

Spinal cord

Spinal column

spinal column

Also called the spine; see **backbone**.

spinal cord

A bundle of nerves that extends from the brain and is housed in the spine. The spinal cord carries nerve impulses to and from the brain.

spine

Also known as the spinal column; see **backbone**.

sprain   (SPRAYN)

The painful wrenching or twisting of a ligament or tendon. Sprains happen most often at the ankle, wrist, and knee joints.

sternum

The flat bone in the center of the chest that forms the central portion of the rib cage. The sternum, or breastbone, also forms the connecting point between the ribs and the clavicle in the shoulder.

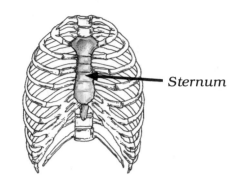

Sternum

stirrup   (STIR-up)

The small bone in the middle ear shaped like a stirrup on a saddle. Also called the stapes (STAY-peez), it is attached to the cochlea of the inner ear. See **middle ear** illustration.

stomach   (STUM-uk)

A digestive organ located in the abdomen below the ribs. In the stomach, food from the esophagus is mixed with enzymes to form a fluid called chyme (KYME). The chyme is released from the stomach into the small intestine, where most of the digestive processes will be completed.

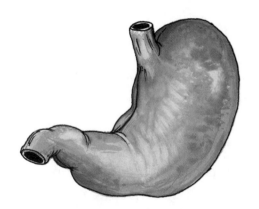

superior vena cava   (soo-PEER-ee-or VEE-nuh KAY-vuh)

A large vein that returns blood to the heart from the upper body. The superior vena cava joins the heart at the right atrium. See **inferior vena cava** illustration.

sweat glands

Glands in the skin that release a mixture of water and salt called sweat or perspiration. This fluid is released when a person is either nervous or uncomfortably warm. The evaporation of sweat from the surface of the skin helps to cool the body.

Synapse

synapse   (SIN-aps)

A very small space at the end of a nerve cell over which chemical signals are passed. These signals stimulate the nearby tissue, which can be muscles, glands, or other neurons.

Talus

talus   (TAY-lus)

The bone at the back of the foot that joins with the two lower leg bones to form the ankle.

taste buds

Tiny sense organs located mainly on the tongue. Taste buds respond to the chemicals in food and send this information to the brain, which then interprets the information as taste. Taste buds are sensitive to sweet, salty, bitter, and sour tastes, depending on where on the tongue they are located.

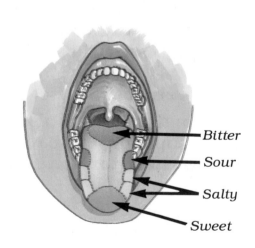

Bitter

Sour

Salty

Sweet

tear

A drop of salty fluid released by the lacrimal (LAK-rih-mal) glands. Tears cleanse the eye and keep it moist.

tear duct

A small tubular passageway from the lacrimal gland to the eye. The lacrimal gland produces tears. Tears move from the gland, through the tear duct, to a tear pool at the corner of the eye near the nose.

teeth

Hard, bony growths rooted in the jaws and used for biting and chewing. Enamel, the hardest substance in the body, covers each tooth. There are thirty-two teeth in a complete set of adult teeth.

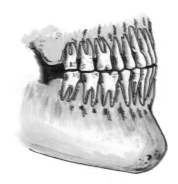

tendon

A tough band of tissue that attaches skeletal muscle to bone. Tendons vary in length, size, and shape, according to the muscle they are connected to.

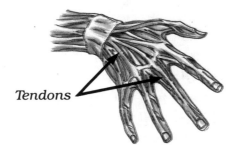

Tendons

thalamus   (THAL-uh-mus)

A large, oval mass of gray matter in the brain above the brain stem. It passes incoming impulses to the cerebral cortex, particularly those of temperature (hot or cold), pain, and touch. The thalamus also helps the body to remain alert.

thigh

The upper leg between the hip and the knee. The bone in the thigh is the femur. There are more than eleven major muscles in the thigh.

thoracic cavity   (thor-AS-ik)

The part of the body that contains the lungs and heart, also called the chest cavity. The thoracic cavity is separated from the abdomen by the diaphragm.

thoracic duct

A large lymph vessel that runs along the spinal column in the thoracic cavity. The thoracic duct forms the main duct of the lymphatic system and empties into a vein in the chest.

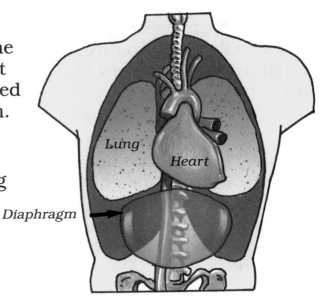

Lung

Heart

Diaphragm

thymus   (THY-mus)

A spongy gland in the upper chest. The thymus gland is large in children, but it shrinks in size with age. Although the exact role of the thymus is unclear, it is thought to play a role in defending against disease.

thyroid   (THY-royd)

The largest of the endocrine glands, located at the base of the neck. The thyroid releases hormones that maintain normal growth and metabolism.

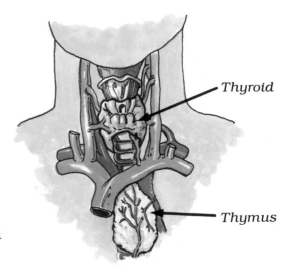

Thyroid

Thymus

tibia   (TIB-ee-uh)

The larger of the two bones in the lower leg. See **fibula** illustration.

tissue   (TISH-yoo)

A group of cells that work together and have the same overall function. There are many types of tissue, and the organs of the body usually contain more than one type. Muscle fibers are composed mainly of muscle tissue and connective tissue.

tonsils   (TAHN-sulz)

Small, rounded lumps of tissue in the throat on either side of the pharynx. The exact job of the tonsils is unclear. They are part of the lymphatic system and appear to help defend against disease.

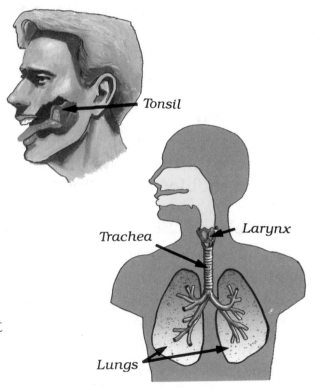

Tonsil

Trachea

Larynx

Lungs

trachea   (TRAY-kee-uh)

A tube through which air flows to the lungs, also called the windpipe. The trachea begins just below the larynx, or voice box. It divides into smaller branches, called bronchi, that connect with the lungs.

triceps   (TRY-seps)

Muscles located in the back of each upper arm. The triceps and biceps work together to move the arms. The triceps contract when the arms are extended, and relax when the arms are flexed. See **biceps** illustration.

45

trunk

The central portion of the body, which includes the chest, abdomen, and pelvic region.

ulna   (UL-nuh)

The inner of the two bones in the forearm. See **radius** illustration.

uvula   (YOO-vyoo-luh)

A small piece of tissue that hangs from the roof of the mouth near the throat. It varies in size and shape from one person to the next.

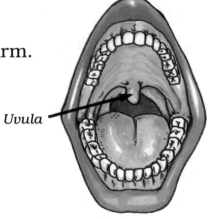

Uvula

veins   (VAYNZ)

The blood vessels that return blood to the heart from the body. Veins have thinner walls than arteries. Veins also have valves that prevent blood from flowing backward.

ventricle   (VEN-trih-kul)

A chamber, or cavity, in the heart. The left ventricle in the heart receives blood from the left atrium, then contracts to drive the blood into the aorta. The right ventricle receives blood from the right atrium and sends it to the pulmonary arteries.

vertebrae   (VER-tuh-bray)

Small, hollow bones that make up the backbone and form a protective covering for the spinal cord. The singular of *vertebrae* is *vertebra.*

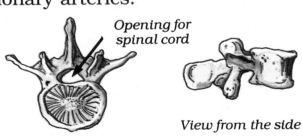

Opening for spinal cord

View from the side

View from above

villi   (VIH-lye)

Tiny folds that line the small intestine. The villi absorb food that has been broken down by digestive juices and pass it into the circulatory and lymphatic systems. The singular of *villi* is *villus*.

virus   (VY-rus)

The tiniest form of living matter. Some viruses are so small that they cannot be seen, even with an optical microscope. Viruses enter the cells of an organism in order to reproduce and, in doing so, cause disease. Illnesses such as colds, flu, and measles are caused by viral infections.

Cold virus invades a cell

vitamin

One of many different substances that are found in foods and are necessary for the body's metabolism to function normally.

vocal cords   (VO-kul kordz)

Two bands of tough, elastic tissue found at the opening of the larynx. The vocal cords vibrate when air from the lungs passes between them, producing sound and enabling humans to speak.

voluntary muscles   (VOL-un-tair-ee)

Muscles that can be controlled by thought or will. Arm and leg muscles are voluntary. The heart muscle is not voluntary.

water

A colorless, tasteless, odorless liquid that is present in all living organisms. The human body is made up of sixty-five percent water.

white blood cell

A white or colorless cell of the blood that has a nucleus but does not contain hemoglobin. There are many kinds of white blood cells, or leukocytes (LOO-kuh-sites), and each has a different function. See **red blood cell** and **immune system** illustrations.

wrist (RIST)

A gliding joint that connects the hand to the forearm.

Bones of the wrist